I0796759

# THE SUNDAY RESET

## Simple Self-Care Rituals to Set Yourself Up for a Successful Week

SOPHIE GOLDING

THE SUNDAY RESET



Text by Caitlin McAllister



An Hachette UK Company
www.hachette.co.uk

Vie Books, an imprint of Summersdale Publishers
Part of Octopus Publishing Group Limited
Carmelite House
50 Victoria Embankment
LONDON
EC4Y 0DZ
UK

www.summersdale.com

This FSC® label means that materials and other controlled sources used for the product have been responsibly sourced

The authorized representative in the EEA is Hachette Ireland, 8 Castlecourt Centre, Dublin 15, D15 XTP3, Ireland (email: info@hbgi.ie)

Printed and bound in China

ISBN: 978-1-83799-739-8
eISBN: 978-1-83799-740-4

# INTRODUCTION

Welcome to your Sunday reset, a day dedicated to making the upcoming week feel organized and achievable. When life becomes chaotic, you can always count on a reset day to help you recharge, to take back control, and to make the week ahead even better than the last.

Throughout this book, you will discover rituals to help you tidy your home, rearrange your calendar, touch base with your goals and more. These ideas have been categorized into mind (blue), body (pink), or life (orange) tips - follow them exactly, or use them as inspiration to design a weekly reset routine that is unique to you.

From streamlining your to-do list, to decluttering your home, to strengthening your mindset for the week ahead, inside this book you'll find everything you need to help you complete your Sunday reset.

## REWIND, REFLECT AND REVIEW

To move into a new week with clarity, it helps to look back on the week before and ask yourself questions to evaluate it, such as:

- What went according to plan?
- Did anything unexpected happen?
- What would you like to do more or less of?
- What were the highlights and lowlights of your week?
- What situation would you have handled differently?

This enlightening mini appraisal can help you select the practices and mindset to bring with you into the next week.

# GIVE YOUR PHONE A TIME-OUT

Around the world, the average person spends around 3 hours and 15 minutes looking at their phone each day, so most of us could benefit from doing a little digital detox during our Sunday reset routine.

A great way to do this (and stick to it) is to put your phone in a drawer for a few hours while you carry on with the activities in this book. After some time, you will likely forget all about it, and your mind will feel clearer and more focused – a welcome reset for your brain.

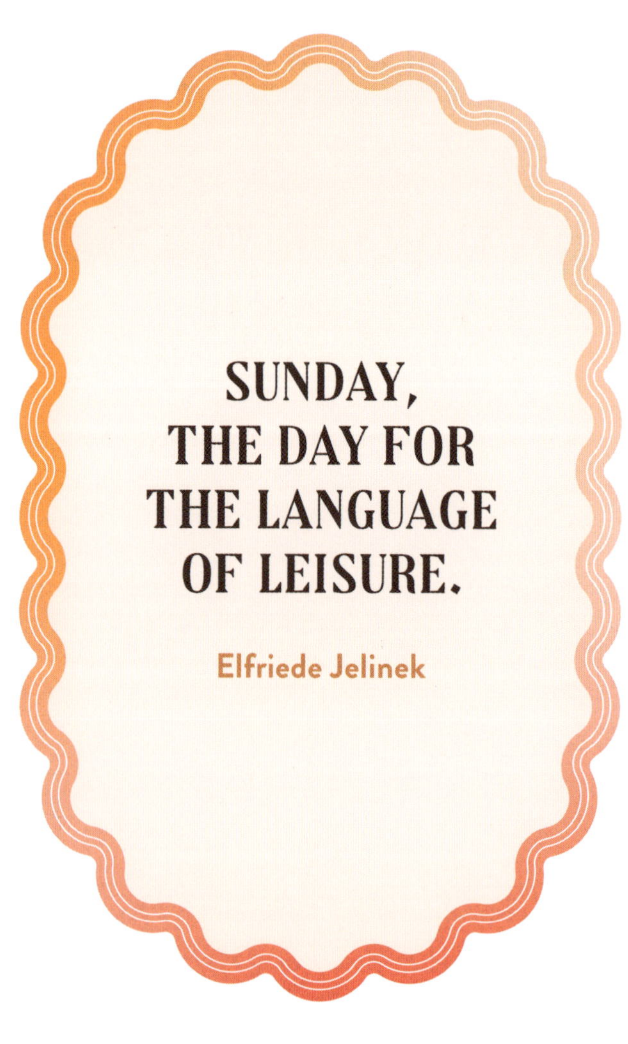

SUNDAY,
THE DAY FOR
THE LANGUAGE
OF LEISURE.

Elfriede Jelinek

# ENJOY A MINDFUL WALK

Whether to reflect on the past week, visualize the week to come, or enjoy alone time in nature, walking has many benefits. It has been shown to help boost energy levels, reduce stress and improve mood, cognition and sleep. Fitting this into your Sunday reset routine is certainly worthwhile.

Make it mindful by paying attention to your steps, noticing colours around you, or breathing in the fresh air as you go. Doing so can help make this less of a brisk, fitness-focused walk, and more of a slow-paced, relaxing stroll to help you recentre and reset.

# WRITE MORNING PAGES

Popularized by the book *The Artist's Way* by Julia Cameron, morning pages are exactly what they sound like: a daily journalling practice done in the morning. This encourages stream-of-consciousness writing, and the idea is to allow everything to escape from your brain before the day has started.

Whether it be angry thoughts, hopes for the day or simply your to-do list, you can write about anything that comes to mind. This is a helpful Sunday reset activity that enables your brain to purge every lingering thought that you don't want to take with you into a new week.

# SORT THROUGH THE MAIL PILE

Other than cards from friends or family members, there are few pieces of mail that people actually enjoy opening. Between utility bills, bank statements and marketing materials, weekly mail can be boring!

However, the more you allow the unopened envelopes to build up, the more time-consuming it will be to sort through junk and regular mail.

Sorting through your mail pile may sound tedious, but you will feel so accomplished afterwards. Deal with the mail that gives you the most anxious feelings first to lighten your mind.

# PRACTISE BREATHWORK

Resetting requires you to turn down the volume on background noise by practising mindful activities. When you carve out focus time, you can more easily see what is causing you stress and visualize how you want the day to go.

To reset the nervous system, practise 4-7-8 breathing, which involves three steps: inhale through the nose for 4 seconds, hold the breath for 7, and finally, exhale through the mouth for 8.

This can help calm the mind, reduce anxiety and train the body to respond to stress in more helpful ways – a handy technique to start your reset day.

BREATHE IN;
BREATHE OUT;

*begin*

# RELIVE LAST WEEK

Visualization exercises are an excellent way to reflect on the past and learn from it. Find a comfortable place to sit, close your eyes, and visualize the week you have just lived. Imagine the main highlights and remember each interaction, decision, success or setback.

Without any judgement, embarrassment or regret, relive the past week to identify anything you believe could be improved.

Would you speak up in that meeting? Spend more time with your children? Call a friend back sooner? This exercise offers an imaginary do-over with the purpose of learning from the past to improve your upcoming week.

**With the new day comes new strength and new thoughts.**

ELEANOR ROOSEVELT

# CLEAR YOUR CALENDAR

In our fast-paced world, we often say "yes" to more than we can handle and overestimate what we can achieve each week. Your Sunday reset is a chance to intentionally arrange activities with future you in mind.

Start by clearing next week's calendar. As you refill the blank spaces with upcoming appointments, remember that *you* get to decide what populates each hour of your time, no one else. Carefully evaluate each calendar entry before adding it to next week's schedule by asking, "Is this an essential task, or something I truly need or want to do?" If not, remove it.

## DO A BRAIN DUMP

Just as you might clear tabs from your browser for a more manageable workload, you can do the same for your mind. Cue the brain dump.

This is a brilliant tool for anyone who feels overwhelmed. To complete a brain dump, sit in a comfortable spot and list everything on your mind, from niggling to-dos, to recurring anxious thoughts. Perhaps you have pantry items to replace, loved ones to call, or projects at work you have been procrastinating on. However tangled your mind feels, this is an easy way to unravel it and feel empowered to tackle next week's priorities.

# GIVE NEXT WEEK A THEME

Choosing a theme isn't just for birthday parties. You can choose a theme for anything in your life to make it more interesting, fun and motivating. While your party theme might be something like "disco" or "floral", your weekly themes can be catered to your goals and specific projects. Some examples might be:

- Deep work
- Radical self-care
- Courage
- Friendship and connection
- Embrace the chaos
- Less consuming, more creating
- Focus, but make it fun

Whatever theme you choose, make it unique to you and something that will give you a boost of motivation for the week ahead.

WHEN LIFE GIVES YOU MONDAY, DIP IT IN GLITTER AND SPARKLE ALL DAY.

Ella Woodward

# STRETCH IT OUT

Few movements feel more satisfying than stretching, particularly after you have been sitting or sleeping in the same position for a long time. Reset your body after sleep by practising a simple stretch routine on a Sunday morning. Move through each part of your anatomy from your feet to your head and gently stretch everything out to feel more flexible and supple.

If you work at a desk on a regular basis, this may be especially important to maintain healthy joints and to help you enjoy the rest of your Sunday reset free from aches and pains.

# APPLY THE 80/20 PRINCIPLE

The 80/20 principle, sometimes called Pareto's Principle, suggests that 80 per cent of outcomes are the result of 20 per cent of inputs. In other words, 80 per cent of success usually comes from 20 per cent of actions. While reviewing your previous week, this can help determine which actions and habits bring the most positive outcomes.

This principle can be applied to any area of life, so reflect on your wins and find what made you feel most happy, successful and confident last week. These discoveries will inform which actions and habits you should take into the following week.

# DO A QUICK-FIRE TIDY

Resetting your space doesn't need to be complicated. You can feel organized and orderly just by doing a quick-fire tidy of your immediate surroundings.

Make your bed. Pick up anything lying on the floor. Put dirty dishes in the sink to soak. Start your day in a positive way by giving your space a speedy spruce-up so you feel refreshed without spending your whole Sunday on this task.

Sometimes you will need to do a deep clean, but other times a quick blitz around the main living areas will suffice and give you the same sense of satisfaction.

# DANCE AND CLEAN

One of the best ways to feel refreshed and reset after a long week is to make your living space sparkling clean. Combining this with a solo dance party could be exactly what you need to clear out the cobwebs in more ways than one.

Put on a playlist of upbeat music and focus on moving your body while cleaning the space around you. This is particularly helpful if you find cleaning tasks mundane, as you can tackle a new section of the room with each new song to keep things interesting. Dance and clean like no one is watching!

HIT THE RESET BUTTON ONCE A WEEK TO REDISCOVER WHAT REALLY *matters*

# SET INTENTIONS

Whenever you are tempted to write a list of lofty goals for next week, remember that defining them as goals in the first place could be a mental barrier. Instead, try defining them as intentions.

While goals tend to feel more long-term, intentions suggest specific actions and a shorter time frame. Whether it's a big or small goal, write this as an intention that specifies how best to achieve it. For example, "Catch up on emails" might become "Set a timer for 15 minutes every morning next week and answer a minimum of five emails before it goes off."

Intentional days create a life on purpose.

ADRIENNE ENNS

# DECLUTTER A PROBLEM AREA

There's probably an area of your home that has been bothering you for a while. Is the garden shed a mess? Do you get annoyed when plastic container lids fall from an overflowing cupboard? Is the stack of paperwork on the kitchen counter slowly becoming a tower?

Choose one area of your home that has been causing frustration recently and declutter it today. Even tidying up a small area, like one drawer, can have a lasting positive impact on the week ahead if it is something that causes you stress on a daily basis.

# MEDITATE

According to studies, meditation has benefits for physical health, such as improved blood pressure and mental health, and can reduce anxiety and depression. Completing a short meditation exercise during a Sunday reset could help release negative feelings from the past week and centre the mind in preparation for the week ahead.

Try this: sit in a quiet place where you feel safe and comfortable, set a timer for 5 minutes, close your eyes, and slowly breathe in and out. You might find it helpful to say a one-word affirmation like "release" or "reset" on the out-breath.

# SAY RESET AFFIRMATIONS

Saying affirmations aloud can be an empowering exercise that helps crystallize the concepts you want to bring into your everyday life. Think up a reset-themed affirmation that helps you move into next week with excitement. As you go about your day, say it aloud at regular intervals.

You could try:

- Next week will be one of my favourite weeks.
- I move into Monday with curiosity and confidence.
- Whenever I want it to, my mind easily finds its way back to happiness.
- I have everything I need to start over.
- My energy is resetting and I'm ready for a great week.

IF YOU DON'T
LIKE SOMETHING,
CHANGE IT.
IF YOU CAN'T
CHANGE IT,
CHANGE YOUR
ATTITUDE.
Maya Angelou

# HAVE AN "EVERYTHING SHOWER"

You might call it an "everything bath" or just a deep clean. Whatever name you give it, this activity is essentially a thorough clean and reset of your body.

During an everything shower, you might use a face scrub to remove impurities from your pores, scrub your skin with a loofah, use a pumice stone on the soles of your feet, apply a deep conditioner to your hair, or shave your legs.

Focus on the areas that need a little extra TLC, and make sure you leave the shower feeling squeaky clean, super fresh and fully reset.

# GET INSPIRED

Resetting your mind sometimes means silencing the noise you usually hear and listening to something different for a change. If you regularly consume content that may be burning you out, seek new inspiration by:

- Reading a book you have been meaning to read for a while.
- Watching an educational YouTube video series.
- Putting on a podcast (there are lots on the topic of resetting).
- Listening to your favourite music artist.

Put last week's busy work schedule, life admin tasks and anything overwhelming aside during your Sunday reset, and do something that inspires you for the week ahead.

# REORDER AND REPLENISH

Are your favourite products running low? If you keep forgetting to pick up replacements, swearing today's the day, your Sunday reset is the time to make good on that promise.

Deodorant, dry shampoo, aftershave, toothpaste, hand cream, toilet roll – whatever is running low, spend 10 minutes on this reset task. Start by doing a quick lap of the house to remind you what products you need to reorder, make a list as you go, and then order them online.

If any are unavailable, set a reminder in your calendar to buy them when you are next near a shop.

# RESET WITH A BEAUTY RITUAL

Just as your everything shower can help you feel refreshed, you may also have some enjoyable beauty rituals that make you feel more confident, helping you tackle next week with ease.

Sunday is the day to indulge, and these simple rituals could provide the relaxation you need to recharge for the week ahead. Pluck those stray eyebrows. Put on the luxury face cream or mask. File your nails. Do red light therapy. Whatever you like to do, set aside some time today to enjoy this process. Treat yourself to feeling good!

SUNDAYS ARE YOUR CHANCE TO *start over*

# MAKE A PROMISE TO YOURSELF

Resetting activities can help clear a clouded mind and reveal any goals that have been forgotten about in the rush of last week. To reconnect with them, make a promise to yourself to act on a goal. This could sound something like:

Next week, I promise to take a step closer to my goal of ............................................................

by ............................................................................................ .

Doing this will help me ...............................................

............................................................................................ .

Phrasing intentions as promises makes them feel more sincere, encouraging you to follow through as you would do for a loved one. This helps to keep you aligned with your goals when life becomes busy.

Be willing
to be a beginner
every single
morning.

MEISTER ECKHART

# ACHIEVE INBOX ZERO

The idea of inbox zero is different for everyone. For some, the goal is to delete all read (and actioned) emails so they see a completely empty inbox. For others, it's to simply reply to every message that makes them feel overwhelmed. If this tip relates to *your* personal inbox, then consider building in time to address other forms of communication, such as text messages. If you would rather focus on work emails, schedule this for Monday morning.

Decide what version of inbox zero feels most helpful to you, and spend some time going through your emails to delete or categorize them.

## PACK YOUR BAG

If you regularly forget things or find yourself rushing to get out of the door each morning, take a few minutes during your Sunday reset to pack a bag so you feel more organized and prepared for the week ahead.

You could:

- Clear out any old receipts.
- Add some energy-boosting snacks and tea bags.
- Pack easy-to-lose items ahead of time, like keys and glasses.
- Restock your daily toiletries, including lip balm, deodorant and hand sanitizer.
- Include a personalized, motivating affirmation to manifest a positive week.

# NOTICE SOMETHING NOVEL

Do you ever get the feeling your days all look the same? If life seems mundane after a busy but predictable week, take a moment during your reset to notice something different or unique about your environment.

You may spend much of your time in this area, so your eyes will have glanced over your surroundings a hundred times. However, identifying something new there can help to disrupt the norm and provide small doses of mindfulness and gratitude.

Wherever you are, challenge yourself to find one thing you haven't noticed before.

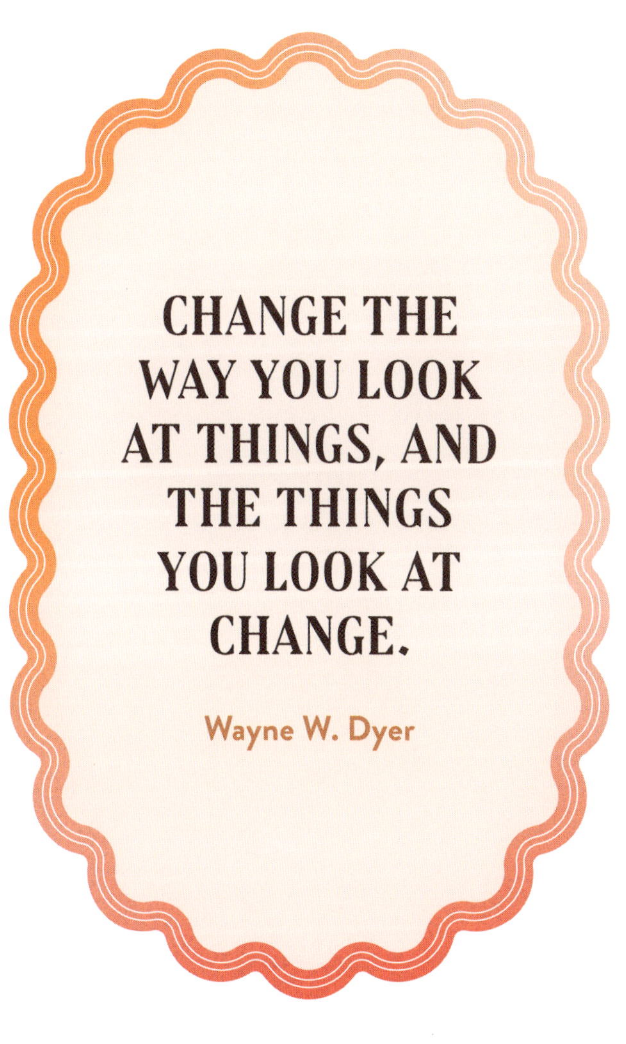
CHANGE THE WAY YOU LOOK AT THINGS, AND THE THINGS YOU LOOK AT CHANGE.
Wayne W. Dyer

# DETOX AND RESET

Our bodies are perfectly designed to detox themselves whenever we consume a little too much of something – within reason, of course. However, you can give your body a helping hand by swapping something you might consider a bad habit (perhaps your fourth coffee of the day) for a healthy option like an antioxidant-rich green juice or a refreshing glass of lemon water.

While a juice cannot truly detox your body, consuming something healthy can help you embrace Sunday reset energy and set you on a positive path for next week.

# UPDATE A MINDFUL FOOD JOURNAL

If your reset goal is to refresh your mindset around healthy eating for next week, having a mindful food journal could help. Whether you are starting one for the first time or updating your current journal, make time for this today.

Start by writing about what you ate last week, without any guilt or regret. Be a curious observer, looking at what you enjoyed, what boosted your energy, or what might have made you feel sluggish.

Based on your findings, write about what nutritious foods you will add to next week's menu. This can shape your shopping list for later.

# CLEAR OUT YOUR FRIDGE

Choosing one area of your home to clean each week can bring a sense of accomplishment, and the fridge can be a practical and satisfying place to start.

Begin by pulling everything out of your fridge temporarily, removing out-of-date food, and preparing anything that can be incorporated into next week's meal plan. Next, wipe up any spills or spatters, and give the shelves a deep clean. Lastly, put everything back in its place, focusing on keeping your most used items in easily accessible areas.

A clean, orderly fridge can streamline your snacking and help you feel more organized at mealtimes.

# PREPARE YOUR MEALS

When healthy choices seem difficult to stick to, or daily cooking becomes tiresome, meal prepping ensures you always have nutritious, easy meals on hand – and you could do this as part of your Sunday reset routine.

Meal prepping usually involves using similar ingredients to cook at least a few days of meals all at once. That way, you can grab one from the fridge or freezer and heat it up any time, without the long cooking process. Examples of easy meals to prepare include overnight oats for breakfasts, a big batch of soup for lunches, and a large portion of lasagne that can be divided up over several days.

# Reset

# ON SUNDAY, THRIVE ON MONDAY

# DO NOTHING

Productivity needn't always be the focus of your reset. Sometimes you can feel recharged by simply doing nothing.

Sit somewhere comfortable, like a cosy corner of your home or a sunny patch in your garden, and simply exist for a while. See what comes to mind.

Rarely do our busy lives allow us to take quiet moments for ourselves, so enjoy this and let your mind wander. Perhaps you will have more reset ideas or think up fun things to try next week.

Enjoy carving out a small slice of your Sunday to do a little bit of nothing.

**There is more to life than increasing its speed.**

MAHATMA GANDHI

# DECLUTTER YOUR TECH

When things feel messy, we are quick to declutter the space around us to feel lighter. Doing the same for your tech items can make using them feel easier and more efficient. If you are on your computer or phone regularly, this could make a huge difference and provide a sense of clarity.

Some things you might consider clearing out include:

- Redundant screenshots saved on your phone.
- Restaurant menu downloads you no longer need.
- Duplicate photos you have taken.
- Old books on your e-reader that you are unlikely to revisit.
- Apps that are negatively affecting your focus.

# AUDIT SOCIAL MEDIA USAGE

Whether you use social media a little or a lot, it undoubtedly influences your thoughts and emotions, and research finds it can cause feelings of anxiety.

To protect your well-being, perform a regular audit of your time spent on each platform. If you believe you're losing too much of your day to social media, reset your usage by downloading an app or computer software that places limits on scrolling – there are many options out there.

Doing this on select Sundays can start to reset your relationship with your phone and interrupt your natural tendency to automatically reach for it.

# FOLLOW POSITIVE INFLUENCES

Social media algorithms are known to show us content that subtly influences our moods without us realizing it. The good news is, we can take back control by clicking the "not interested" button on any posts we no longer wish to see, and unfollowing accounts that contribute to negative thoughts. Instead, we have the choice to seek out content that makes us feel happy and inspired.

This is a great Sunday reset activity that can send you into the next week surrounded only by uplifting and empowering content. By following exclusively positive influences and being mindful of the posts you engage with, you can reset your headspace.

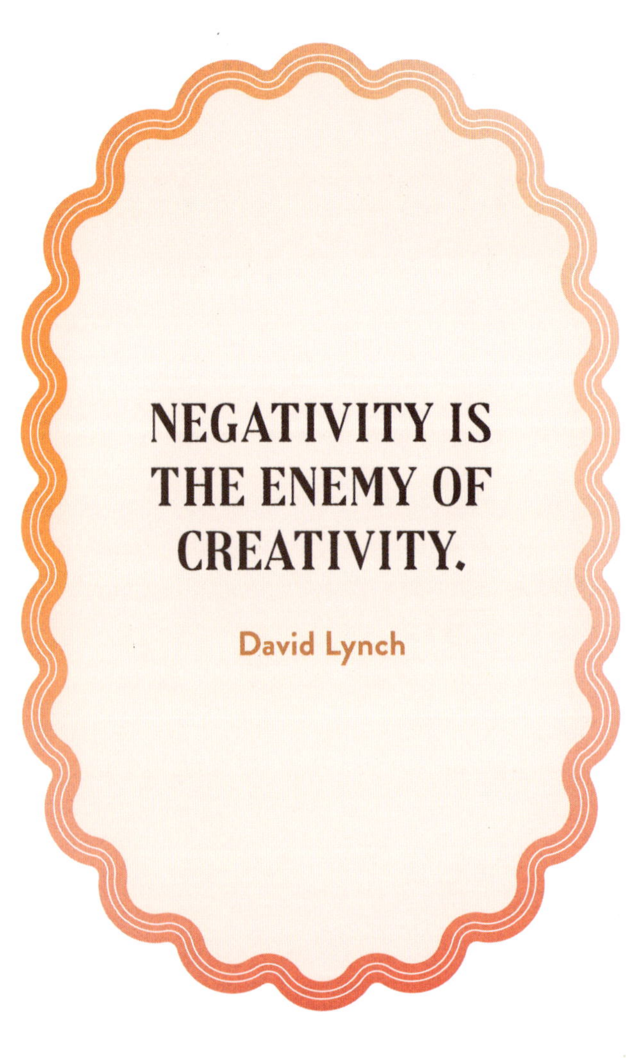
NEGATIVITY IS THE ENEMY OF CREATIVITY.
David Lynch

# COMPLETE AN INTENSIVE SKINCARE ROUTINE

After a busy week, swap your quick face wash for a more intensive skincare routine to help you feel refreshed and rejuvenated.

Sunday is your day to do all the skincare activities that take too long during the week. Double cleanse, put on a pore-clearing face mask, apply your favourite serums, spend time using a skin roller, apply under-eye patches, and anything else you love to do but rarely find the time for.

Wash away last week and make sure your skin is fresh and ready for Monday morning.

# WORK YOUR CONFIDENCE MUSCLES

Self-confidence is a muscle we can build – we just need to remember to exercise it. Your Sunday reset is a great time to reset your confidence by saying goodbye to anything embarrassing, awkward or negative from the past week.

Do one small thing today to improve your confidence; write an affirmation about your inner beauty on a sticky note on your mirror, go somewhere new on public transport, or perhaps even take yourself out on a solo date!

Whatever will recalibrate your self-confidence, factor this into your day. You have nothing to lose and everything to gain.

# REVIEW YOUR FINANCES

Few people look forward to budgeting their finances. Though ignoring it can be less stressful in the short term, it can lead to further financial worries down the line. A regular review and reset of your budgets and saving goals could help you feel more organized, in control and calm about your financial outlook.

Incorporate some number crunching into your Sunday reset, and future you will thank you for it. Make it fun by putting on relaxing music and drinking your favourite tea. You could even do this alongside a friend for support. After a few weeks, this will become easier and less stressful.

# SCAN YOUR BODY

A body scan can help identify where in your body needs some TLC.

Start by sitting or lying down somewhere quiet where you can concentrate. Close your eyes and focus on the very top of your head. Scan down your face, neck, back and torso, arms, hips, thighs, calves and finally, feet. As you scan down each area of your body, think about whether you feel any pain, discomfort, tiredness, or any little niggles that might need your attention.

This can help you discover any problem areas to stretch out and show a little extra care to next week.

THE PERFECT TIME DOES NOT EXIST;

*Start today*

# PLAN YOUR WEEKLY WORKOUTS

Sticking to an exercise routine is easier when you plan ahead, so take time to think about the workouts you would like to do next week to stay on track with your fitness goals.

Decide which days you will exercise and what workouts you'd like to do, whether that's lifting weights at the gym, walking, yoga, or anything else!

You could also choose what you're going to wear, what equipment you'll need, and the details of your workout, such as the routine you're going to follow. Planning this removes any mental barriers so you feel ready for your workouts next week.

**Success is to wake up each morning and consciously decide that today will be the best day of your life.**

KEN POIROT

# REVAMP YOUR BEDROOM

Your Sunday reset is a great time to revamp your bedroom. It can be fun to spruce up your space, so take the opportunity during your reset to make your bedroom feel more relaxing and inviting. You could:

- Add a photo frame featuring loved ones to make the space more personal.
- Arrange decorative cushions on your bed for additional comfort.
- Move your furniture around for a totally new look.
- Switch your bedcover to a new colour or pattern.
- Move your phone charger elsewhere and make your bedroom a tech-free zone.

# MAKE A WEEKLY VISION BOARD

Vision boards are an effective way to stay aligned with your goals, and their potential is backed by research. These inspiring and motivating images and words can become a visual representation of what you are striving to achieve next week.

Whether you make this on a piece of card to stick on your wall or create a wallpaper for your phone each week, this is a creative way to ensure your goals and dreams are always at the forefront of your mind.

Make the process fun by playing music in the background, and spend 30 minutes creating your vision board for next week.

# TRY SOLUTION-FOCUSED JOURNALLING

Some people love free-flow journalling to see what emerges from the depths of their mind. If this is not for you, solution-focused journalling may be the answer, as it involves writing down a problem you want to solve.

Perhaps you clash with another personality type at work, lack time in your week to see friends, or are unsure where to go on your next family holiday. Whatever has been weighing on you, this is a great way to lay the problem out in words and journal your way to a solution that will help reset your worried mind.

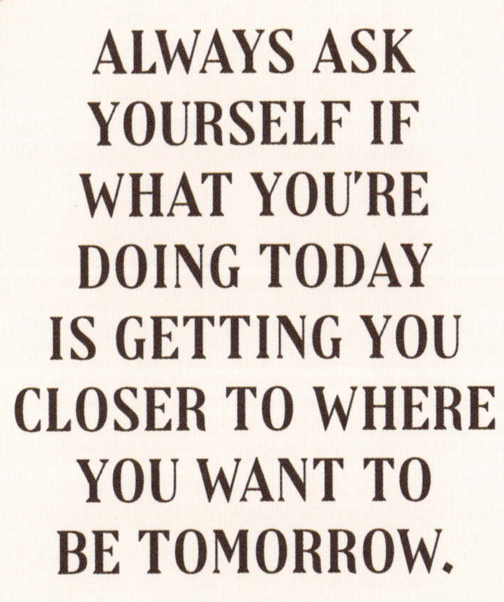

**ALWAYS ASK YOURSELF IF WHAT YOU'RE DOING TODAY IS GETTING YOU CLOSER TO WHERE YOU WANT TO BE TOMORROW.**

Paulo Coelho

# GIVE YOURSELF A MASSAGE

If you don't have time for a professional massage, there are ways to improve tight muscles yourself. Your body scan exercise (see page 54) could help alert you to any problem areas, so start by identifying where the issues lie and set aside 10 minutes during your Sunday reset routine to focus on these muscles.

Whether you feel tightness in your lower back, neck or shoulders, or you simply want to treat yourself to a foot massage, use body oil on the area and apply gentle pressure to relieve any tightness or pain.

Prepare weary muscles for whatever next week brings!

# CALL A FRIEND

Connecting with friends is not only a fun way to spend your time, it also has mental health benefits, like contributing to a sense of belonging, boosting happiness and lowering stress.

Spend time re-establishing connections with your closest friends and family members, especially if you haven't spoken to them in a while. Catch up on what has been happening in each other's lives and enjoy the feeling of satisfaction that comes from chatting with your nearest and dearest.

Whether you call, text or see them in person, make time during your Sunday to connect with the people who leave you feeling uplifted and loved.

# GET OUT OF YOUR USUAL ENVIRONMENT

A change of scenery every now and then can do wonders for your mental health, so if you are struggling to maintain momentum during your Sunday reset, go somewhere you don't see every day.

This is particularly important if you spend a lot of time at home or in the same space, as getting some distance and a new perspective can allow you to more clearly see the areas of life that need to be reset.

# SHOW YOUR HAIR SOME LOVE

If you have been neglecting your locks for a while now, your Sunday reset is the ideal time to give them some attention. No matter what length, colour or style you prefer, there are always ways to indulge and put your hair front and centre for a change.

Here are a few ways you could do this:

- Do a deep conditioning hair mask.
- Book in a much-needed trim.
- Give hair a day off from heat styling.
- Apply a nourishing oil to the ends.
- Give yourself a scalp massage.

NEXT WEEK
DESERVES
YOUR FULL

*attention*

# MAKE A SPARE TIME PLAN

We often forget to schedule fun, instead opting to fill spare time with an overspill of practical or productive tasks. During your Sunday reset, consider where in next week's schedule you could find pockets of free time for fun.

Could that 10-minute break be a chance to read a few pages of your book? Could that spare hour be an opportunity to meet a friend for coffee?

Create a spare time plan and add ideas whenever you feel inspired. Each time you reset your calendar, consult the list to fill your free time with fun and mini adventures.

**When you can and as you can, in ways that feel loving, make time and space for yourself.**

TRACEE ELLIS ROSS

# STOCK YOUR PANTRY

There is something calming and exciting about seeing your cupboards and fridge filled up with healthy food and fun snacks, so this is a great activity for your Sunday reset when supplies have dwindled throughout the week.

Take time to write out everything you need; check any grocery lists you continuously add to and look through your kitchen to see what may be running low before you hit the shops for your grocery haul.

A fully stocked pantry can make you feel organized for the week ahead.

## RESET FOR OTHERS

Sometimes reset routines involve resetting for someone (or something) other than ourselves. Here are a few ways you could help others reset on a Sunday:

- Plan out your kids' packed lunches for next week.
- Add more food to the automatic cat feeder.
- Take one thing off your partner's plate for next week.
- Water and repot your houseplants.

These reset tasks are acts of kindness, so while you reset the routines of others in your life, don't forget to enjoy the mood-boosting properties of doing something nice for someone else!

# REVIEW YOUR SAVES

Do you click save on life hack ideas on social media? Fold down the corner of recipe pages? Or note down words you want to look up the meaning of later? We all have a series of tabs open in our brain at the end of each week, reminding us of things we saved for later.

Your Sunday reset is officially “later”, so it’s time to either use them or lose them.

Visit all the places you tend to collect things, and for each, decide whether it’s worth keeping or if it was a spur-of-the-moment save you no longer need.

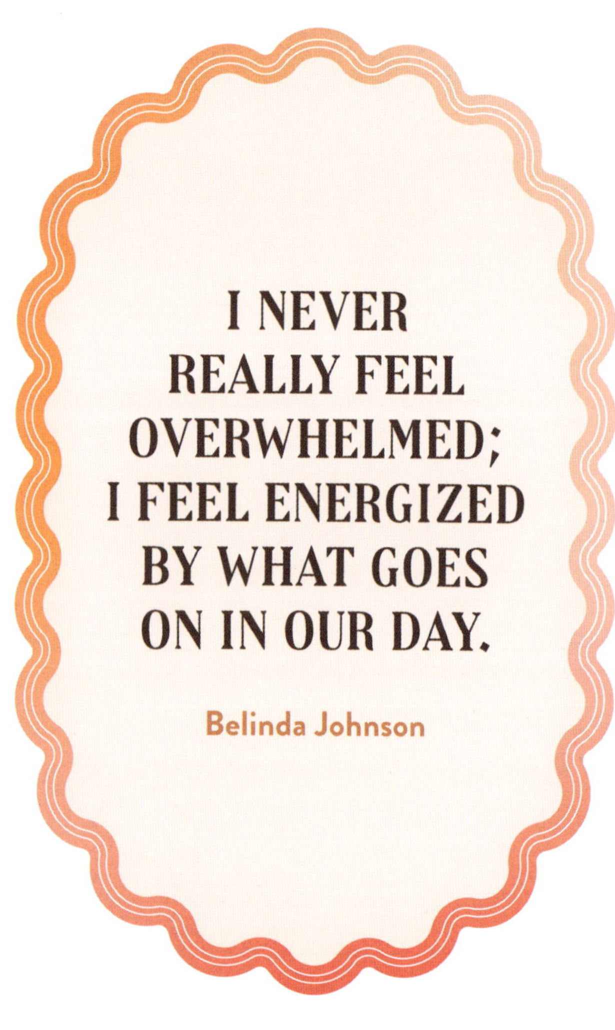

I NEVER
REALLY FEEL
OVERWHELMED;
I FEEL ENERGIZED
BY WHAT GOES
ON IN OUR DAY.

Belinda Johnson

# SET A WEEKLY STEP GOAL

Step goals are a helpful way to get your body moving, particularly if you have a sedentary job or sit in a classroom all day. While a common daily goal is 10,000 steps, everyone requires a different amount, so decide what works for you.

Another option is a weekly step goal, which accounts for inevitable daily fluctuations. This means, if you don't hit your target one day, you could balance this out later in the week. Take notice of your average weekly steps during your reset to see what you could change next week, or to celebrate an active week.

# REVIEW YOUR BIGGEST GOALS

Sunday resets are great for getting lots of little tasks done, but remember to also zoom out, take stock, and check in with your big goals. Regularly reviewing goals is the best way to stay focused and take at least one action, no matter how small.

If your goal is to eat healthier, spending your entire Sunday cleaning your home will not move the needle. Similarly, if you crave an organized, tidy home, spending your Sunday meal prepping won't help you achieve this.

Check in with your biggest goals to keep your reset moving in the right direction.

# STREAMLINE YOUR SUCCESS

While thinking about big goals, take a minute to make any changes to your routine, schedule or environment that might support these in the week ahead.

Do you need to put your dumbbells in a visible place to prompt a workout? Could you place your daily vitamins by the kettle to remind you to take them while making your morning coffee? Can any irrelevant tasks be removed from next week's schedule to make room for actions that will bring you closer to your biggest goal?

Reshape your life to make achieving your dreams more achievable.

# REORGANIZE YOUR WARDROBE

Seasons and trends change constantly, so a wardrobe review should be a regular part of your reset. Go through your clothes and ask questions like:

- Do I still love this item?
- Is this item appropriate for the weather right now? If not, can it be stored elsewhere?
- Could someone else get more wear out of this? If so, should I donate it?

The 333 wardrobe hack could help; this challenge suggests dressing with only 33 items (including accessories) for three months, which means you have a handy capsule wardrobe for the whole season before switching it up.

A SUNDAY RESET IS YOUR

*head start*

FOR THE WEEK

# REVERSE-ENGINEER YOUR GOALS

During your goal check-in, one way to ensure you are moving forwards is, ironically, to work backwards. Take 10 minutes to imagine yourself working backwards from your end goal.

For example, if you want to write a book, choose a launch date and work backwards to identify the steps:

- I will share the book with my friends and family by...
- I will finish the first draft by...
- I will write X words every month
- I will write the outline by...

Big goals can seem daunting when stretched out before you, but finding an endpoint and working backwards makes them more manageable.

**People with goals succeed because they know where they're going.**

EARL NIGHTINGALE

# HIT UNSUBSCRIBE

A satisfying task for your Sunday reset is to unsubscribe from those pesky junk emails that frustrate you. We all get so many emails each day, so instead of deleting them, pick out the ones that you never read and take 15 minutes to scroll to the bottom of each one and unsubscribe.

This is a great favour for your future self and will make next week feel that little bit lighter! Every few Sundays, delete more and more until you can finally say goodbye to annoying, pointless emails.

# DECLUTTER YOUR PROJECTS

We all have hidden projects we don't realize are overwhelming us, and your reset day is the perfect time for a clear-out. Projects are things that take days, weeks or months, rather than simple one-and-done tasks that are easily completed.

Adding something like "clear out the attic" is not a quick-win task; this is a project. If you have hidden projects on your to-do list, there are two things you can do:

1. Break them down into smaller, more actionable steps, or
2. Get rid of them completely.

Declutterring hidden projects helps you feel lighter and refreshed for next week.

# AUDIT YOUR BIG LIFE GOALS

Just as you have decluttered your small projects, you can also audit and declutter your bigger life goals. The milestone you have been trying to hit since last year may not feel as important now as it did when you started, so take a few minutes to think about your life goals and decide if they are still a priority.

Instead of mindlessly copying old tasks into future to-do lists to achieve goals you are no longer passionate about, use your Sunday reset to mindfully consider what you *really* want.

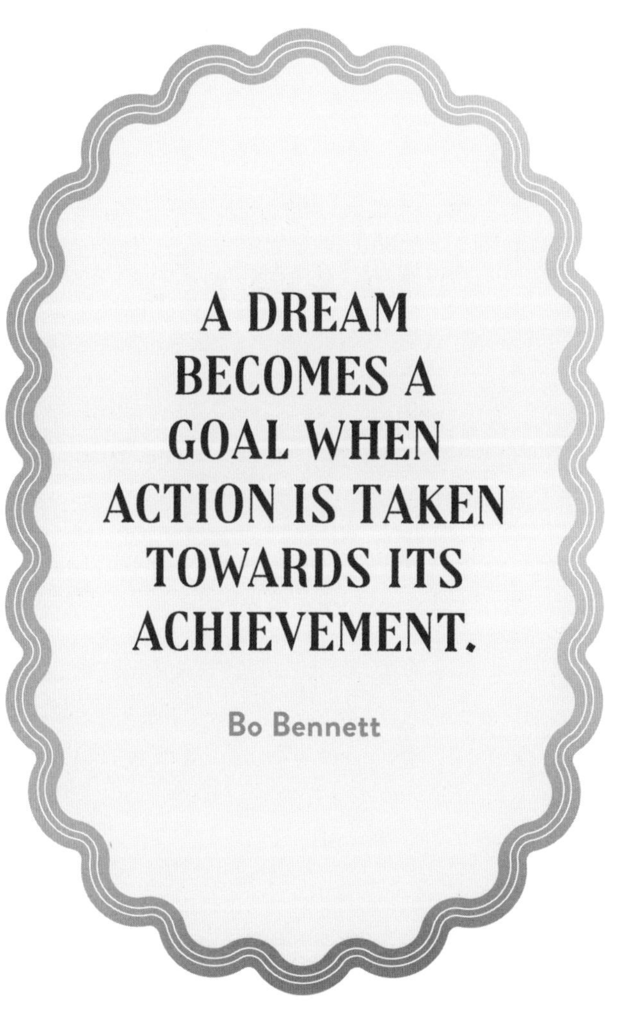

A DREAM BECOMES A GOAL WHEN ACTION IS TAKEN TOWARDS ITS ACHIEVEMENT.

Bo Bennett

# ENERGIZE TO EMPOWER

If Sundays make you feel sluggish and sleepy, and you want to change this, do something energizing today to empower you for the week ahead.

This can be anything that's personally energizing to you; put on your favourite upbeat song to dance to, read a motivating self-development book, go for a jog, stretch your body, say "hello" to strangers on a walk. Anything that makes you feel lively, positive and energized, take just a few minutes to add this into your Sunday reset and boost your positive energy for the week ahead.

# RELAX AND RECENTRE

Boosting your energy during your reset is helpful, but don't forget Sunday is also a day of rest, so make time for this, too. Choose something that relaxes you.

Do you love watching cooking shows? Do you feel relaxed after painting or doing an adult colouring book? Does reading next week's horoscope make you feel calmer about what's to come? Or do you simply need a few minutes to close your eyes and take a nap?

Whatever feels personally relaxing to you, take some time to incorporate this into your day.

# SET TIMELY REMINDERS

Turn goals and aims into tangible tasks that you will get done, even when you are busy. Go through the brain dump list you made earlier (see page 15), and the tasks you identified while reverse-engineering your goals (see page 78).

From these lists, set little reminders throughout next week that will prompt you to take action on something that is a priority for you. This is your chance to make it happen, rather than letting another week slip by without action.

# BOOK IMPORTANT APPOINTMENTS

Your Sunday reset is an excellent time to schedule those appointments or make the calls you have been procrastinating on. Here are some ideas:

- Do you need to set up a recurring prescription?
- When was the last time you booked teeth cleaning at the dentist?
- Do you need to make an appointment with the bank?
- Are you in charge of making a restaurant reservation for your friend's birthday?
- Should you book your car in for a service?

If any of your appointment bookings need to be made on a weekday, set a reminder for Monday morning to get these done.

# RESET YOUR LIFE TO LIGHTEN YOUR *mind*

# FOCUS ON FEELINGS

If last week was stressful in any way, use your Sunday reset to focus on the feelings you would like to bring into next week instead.

Calm, organized, at ease, grateful, focused; whatever feelings would help you most, choose one or two and think of a few ways you could enhance these in the week ahead.

For example, feelings of connection could be created by spending more time with loved ones and less time scrolling social media.

**You only get one life, so you might as well feel all the feelings.**

GRETA GERWIG

# DO THAT TASK

We all have *that* task. The one that has been looming over us for weeks, months or even years. It is usually something that causes us to feel guilt, sadness, frustration, worry or dread when we think about it, and these feelings may grow depending on how long it has been lingering.

The sooner you tackle it, the less scary it will seem, and the sooner you will feel relieved to have it over with.

Find the thing on your list that you have been procrastinating on and set a timer during your reset to finally begin to face it.

# DO FUTURE YOU A FAVOUR

Sunday resets are about adjusting things to make next week easier, so this is a great time to do a small favour for your future self.

Look at next week's to-do list and calendar, and ask yourself what one thing would make next week easier?

You could meal prep for the days you're out and about, cancel the subscription that automatically renews next week so it's off your mind, or charge your phone in another room to stop you from scrolling first thing in the morning.

Whatever will make next week easier, take one small action today.

# PREPARE FOR SETBACKS

Feeling fully reset means feeling ready for anything, including setbacks like car trouble, friends mixing up the days of your coffee catch-up, and last-minute presentations to prepare for.

Things come up unexpectedly, and that's OK. Getting frustrated when plans can't go ahead does not help, so prepare for setbacks in advance by doing any checks you can ahead of time. You could ensure your car has enough fuel, confirm plans with friends, or double-check your calendar in case you missed anything important. Take just a few minutes to anticipate any setbacks that might be coming your way next week.

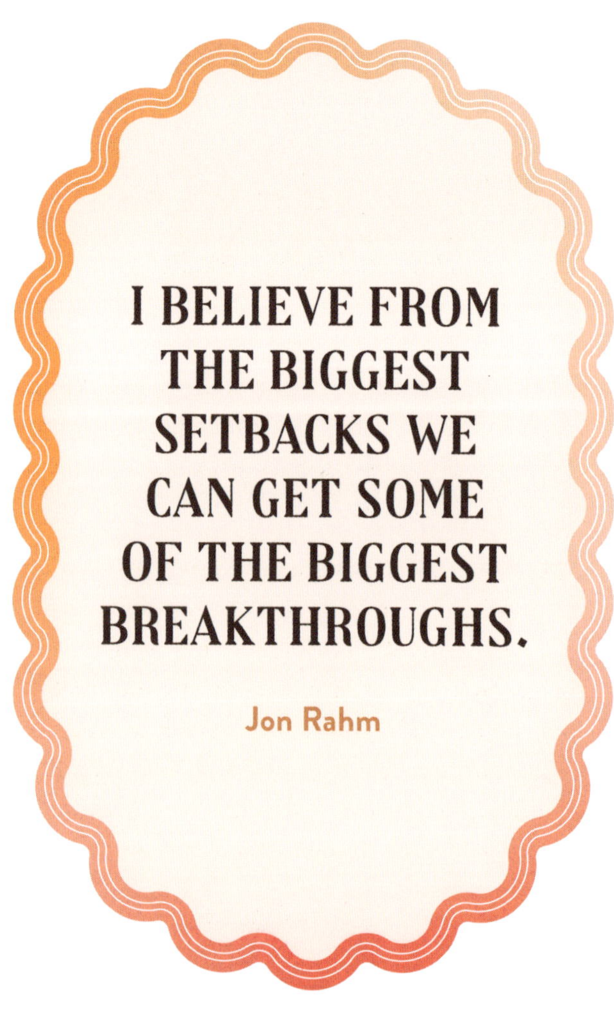
I BELIEVE FROM THE BIGGEST SETBACKS WE CAN GET SOME OF THE BIGGEST BREAKTHROUGHS.
Jon Rahm

# BEAUTIFY AND REFRESH

What better way to reset than by planning or booking all the grooming and beauty appointments you may have been neglecting recently? Here are some ideas:

- Book to get your colour redone before an upcoming event.
- Schedule your regular brow appointment.
- Tackle tight shoulder muscles by booking a massage.
- Arrange a pedicure before your summer holiday.
- Book a facial to feel refreshed.

Whether it's regular bodily maintenance or it's something to treat yourself, Sunday is a great day to plan or book your appointments.

# GET GROUNDED

Many people engage in grounding practices to help with everything from blood flow to mood to sleep quality. This involves having your body make contact with the natural ground, such as taking off your shoes and walking on grass.

During your Sunday reset, try a grounding exercise to bring you back to centre. You could walk barefoot on the beach if you live near the ocean, or simply lie down in your garden. Find somewhere you can connect with nature directly and spend time doing this to balance out your screen time and reap the resetting benefits for next week.

# DO A LIFE ADMIN BLITZ

Life admin tasks are easy to ignore, and they build up over time. Every so often we need to buckle down and move some of them from pending to done. Here are some ideas:

- Change the batteries in electronics that are running slow.
- Do laundry.
- Mend any items that need repairs.
- Pay outstanding bills.
- Back up important documents on your computer or phone.

If these tasks feel tedious, do something to make them more enjoyable, like putting on an interesting podcast or listening to uplifting music while you work.

# PLAN YOUR OUTFITS

If you want to feel extra organized for next week, plan your outfits ahead of time and arrange them in a way that makes you excited to wear them.

Start by checking the weather to prepare for all eventualities. Then, decide which outfits work for each day, such as a smart suit for meetings, or comfortable shorts for the gym. Next, group each piece together so everything matches in colour and style. Lastly, hang them together in the wardrobe and place accompanying accessories in pockets or on the hangers.

Reset these each Sunday to remove decision fatigue from next week.

Today

IS THE ONLY
DAY WORTH
THINKING
ABOUT

# DO A GUIDED MEDITATION

One practice that can support your Sunday reset is a guided meditation to improve readiness for the week ahead. There are lots of these available online or in apps, and you can have them playing aloud or in your headphones.

A guided meditation will usually walk you through the process of calming your thoughts, help you focus on a particular affirmation, and could even promote empowering weekly reset energy. Find one that specifically supports things like resetting or restarting and see if this helps you effectively prepare for next week.

Nobody can go back and start a new beginning, but anyone can start today and make a new ending.

MARIA ROBINSON

# INGREDIENT PREP

Meal prepping is a fantastic way to stick to healthy eating habits, ensuring there are always nutritious meals in the fridge. Your Sunday reset is a great time for this so you have a week's worth of healthy meals prepped and ready for you and your family.

If you want more variety throughout the week, another option is to do ingredient prep instead. Chop up vegetables, cook meats, boil potatoes, and prepare anything that makes it easy to throw loose ingredients into a pan. You can cook up something quick and easy, and switch up the spices and sauces.

# CHECK IN WITH YOUR ACCOUNTABILITY PARTNER

An accountability partner is someone you trust who checks in with you to find out if you have done what you said you would. Having someone do this can help to keep you on track with the tasks you want to tick off and the goals you want to achieve.

Sunday is a perfect day to check in with them, so let them know what you managed to get done this week, or if you came across any barriers. Do the same for them if they need accountability.

Resetting your week together can make the process much more fun.

# TIDY YOUR BEDROOM

Having a tidy bedroom is a great way to feel organized and ready to relax.

Spend 10 minutes picking up each item and returning it to its rightful place in the room; clothes on the floor go in the hamper, jackets thrown on the bed get hung up in the wardrobe, earrings strewn across your nightstand go back into the jewellery box.

This simple act can help you to feel much more settled so you can enjoy the rest of your Sunday.

ACCOUNTABILITY
BREEDS
RESPONSE-
ABILITY.

Stephen R. Covey

# RECENTRE WITH TAI CHI

Tai chi is a great activity to promote relaxation and mindfulness to reset for the week ahead.

This Chinese martial art involves a series of slow-moving poses that can help calm your body and steady your thoughts so you feel ready to take on anything life throws at you next week. Tai chi has many benefits, including strengthening your muscles, improving balance and reducing stress. You might find classes on a Sunday in your local area, but if not, there are many videos online that will show you how to practise this.

# BE GRATEFUL

A regular gratitude practice can help you feel more optimistic and notice the good things around you. When planning for a great week ahead, include some gratitude exercises to set you up for success.

For example, close your eyes and think about what happened last week that you feel grateful for, or write them down in a list. This could be anything: long-awaited plans with friends, unexpectedly finishing work early, getting tickets to see your favourite artist perform.

Focusing on feelings of gratitude can help boost your positivity.

# CLEAR THE CLOTHING PILE

Most of us have a wardrobe for clean clothes and a laundry hamper for clothes that have been worn, but sometimes we develop a pile of clothing in the corner of the bedroom that sits somewhere in between: worn, but not unclean enough to require washing.

Things like jeans or a hoodie could be worn multiple times, so eventually we start to build a pile of miscellaneous clothes that exist in laundry limbo. Reset that pile by deciding if they go back into the wardrobe, or if they should be added to the next washing load.

# PREPARE YOUR SNACKS

If you struggle with spontaneous munching on sweets, salty foods and other snacks you would rather avoid, don't quit snacking altogether. Instead, make healthy snacks more accessible and enticing.

Just as you would meal prep to ensure you have healthy meals available (see page 43), you can also do this with your snacks to make them easy to grab instead of reaching for unhealthy ones. You could whip up some protein balls or create your own trail mix using your favourite nuts, seeds and dried fruit.

Reset your snacking habits to make healthy eating a breeze next week.

# A new beginning

**IS MERELY HOURS AWAY**

# EXPLORE A NEW HOBBY

It's far too easy to procrastinate on starting a hobby, so as part of your Sunday reset, set aside some time to get curious. Research shows hobbies are good for our mental and physical health as well as our mood, so there are many benefits to dedicating time to trying something new.

You might choose to research a new class in your area, purchase the supplies you need to get started, or look for local meet-ups of other people already doing this. Find a way to take the first step towards making this exciting hobby a part of your routine from here on out.

**Every sunset is an opportunity to reset. Every sunrise begins with new eyes.**

RICHIE NORTON

# CHANGE YOUR BEDSHEETS

If changing your bedsheets wasn't on your list of cleaning or laundry tasks during your Sunday reset, now is a great time to replace them so you start a new week in a clean bed. Enjoy the feeling of crisp, comfy sheets and that fresh-linen smell that everyone loves.

As an added bonus, why not pick out some fresh new pyjamas to wear too? Clean bedding and fresh pyjamas make a dreamy pairing.

This is an easy win that can make bedtime feel like sleeping on a cloud – the perfect way to drift off after a big reset day.

## READ TO RESET

Reading during your downtime is not only a handy way to get more reading done, it can also help quieten your mind, allow you to spend a few mindful moments alone, and still your thoughts.

Whether you want to be motivated by interesting ideas or escape into a fictional world, reading can often be more of a relaxing and mindful activity than watching TV or scrolling on your phone.

Set aside at least 10 minutes during your Sunday reset to get lost in a great story and feel inspired and refreshed afterwards.

# BE PRESENT AND CONNECT

Few Sunday routines will be successful or enjoyable if they are spent zoning out, doomscrolling or binge-watching TV shows. Being present and connecting with others really is the best way to embrace the reset feeling.

Swap watching your usual TV shows for a documentary with a friend, and chat about its meaning afterwards. Or swap social media scrolling for a phone call with your grandparent. Exchange video game time for a chat with your partner where you check in about what is on your to-do list next week, your worries, and what you are looking forward to.

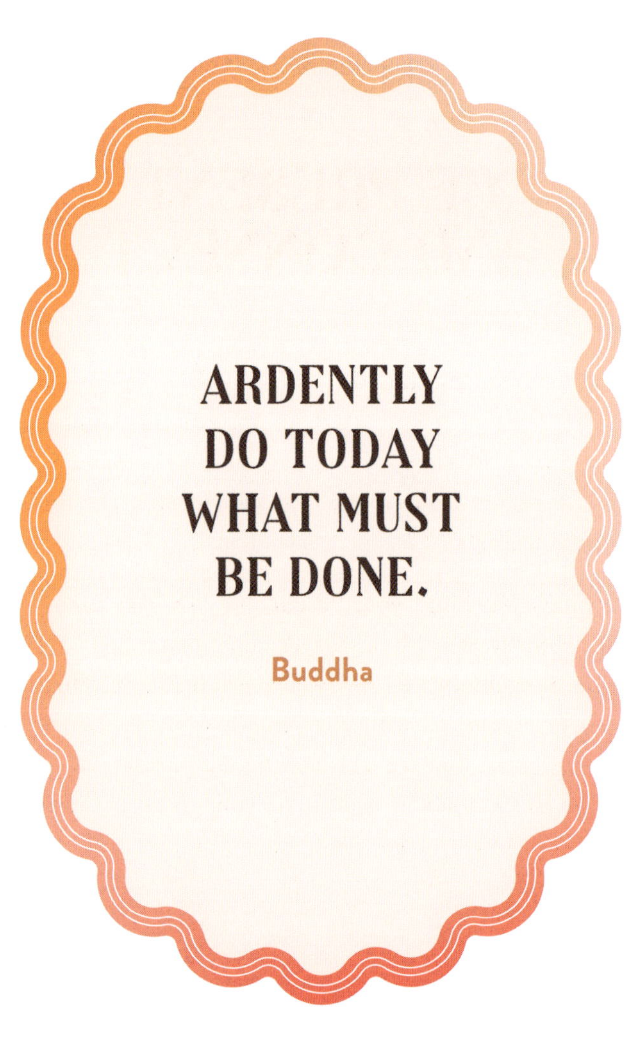

ARDENTLY DO TODAY WHAT MUST BE DONE.

Buddha

# RESET THE SCENTS AROUND YOU

Have you ever noticed how certain scents hold different emotions for us? They can evoke feelings of sleepiness, motivation, and even bring up nostalgic memories. Take time to reset the smells around your home for the week ahead. You could:

- Place fresh flowers in your living room to create a welcoming scent for visitors.
- Refill your automatic coffee maker and wake up to the invigorating smell of coffee.
- Add a diffuser to your bedside with lavender aromatherapy oils to promote sleep.

There are many ways to incorporate scents into your home and make your life smell beautiful.

# RESET YOUR SLEEP ROUTINE

There are many ways to promote sleep, so if you regularly struggle to get a decent slumber and reset for the week ahead, Sunday is a great time to get to bed earlier than usual and take considered action to improve sleep.

Here are a few things to try:

- Fill your room with sleep-inducing aromatherapy oils.
- Dim your lights several hours before bed.
- Invest in blackout blinds or a sleep mask to block light.
- Turn down your thermostat, as a cooler temperature can help promote sleep.
- Wear earplugs in bed to shut out loud noises.

# RESET YOUR ALARM

When the time comes to reset your alarm clock for next week, do this with restfulness in mind.

If you have been waking up before the sun for the last week, consider whether getting a few more hours of slumber is possible, and whether it could help your body and mind to feel more rested and ready for a great week.

Sleep is important, and research recommends adults get over 7 hours for optimum rest time. If you decide to set your alarm later, consider getting an early night to help you feel more energized and reset come Monday morning.

# TRY PROGRESSIVE MUSCLE RELAXATION

Progressive muscle relaxation is an excellent tool to promote mindfulness and relaxation during your Sunday reset ritual. You can do this by lying in a comfortable spot, closing your eyes, and slowly focusing on relaxing the muscles in each part of your body, one by one. Start from the top of your head and work your way down.

You can use this tool any time if you want to feel more relaxed, but doing it during your Sunday reset is an effective way to help you feel more present in your body for the following week.

**MOVE YOUR BODY,
CHANGE YOUR ENERGY,
SHAKE UP THE SPACE;**

# START TODAY

Think back to the goals and tasks you have planned for next week (see page 92), and consider how you could start today, rather than tomorrow. You can look at this as doing your future self a favour, or just getting a head start on next week. Either way, it's about doing one thing today to create a mindset that encourages immediate action rather than procrastination.

So often we say we will start on Monday, or next week, or next year, and so on. Change that today by taking action on something right now.

If you don't see
a clear path for
what you want,
sometimes you have
to make it yourself.

MINDY KALING

# VISUALIZE YOUR PERFECT WEEK

Visualization is a brilliant tool to help you focus on what you want out of life. Sit with your eyes closed and visualize the perfect version of next week. This can help you go into the week excited and ready to hit the ground running.

Visualize yourself overcoming obstacles, breezing through to-do lists, spending time with those who matter, experiencing feelings of accomplishment, and celebrating success after the next seven days have passed.

Making visualization part of your reset routine is a fun and empowering way to feel prepared for the week ahead, and to tell yourself, "I've got this."

# THE END

A Sunday reset can be the ritual you need to bring focus and purpose to your weekend, leaving you with a simple, streamlined roadmap for the week ahead. By committing to this routine, you can start every week with renewed energy and a more positive outlook. Return to these tips midweek if you need to, and use them as tools to refresh your mind, recharge your body and reorganize your life whenever things become overwhelming.

Mindless activities allow weekends to slip through your fingers, so act intentionally to bring you closer to the things you really want in life. Take charge of your time and feel excited for the week ahead by completing your Sunday reset.

**HAPPY RESETTING!**

## HOW TO ROMANTICIZE YOUR LIFE

### Joyful Tips and Advice to Elevate Every Day

**Sophie Golding • Hardback**

**ISBN: 978-1-83799-466-3**

Learn how to elevate your everyday with this stunning guide to finding joy in everything you do. With the help of this book, you'll soon be on the path to a life that's filled with gratitude, self-kindness, and simple, magical moments.

## GOOD MORNING RITUALS

Daily Rituals to Help You Rise and Shine

**Miranda Moore • Hardback**

**ISBN: 978-1-80007-926-7**

Whether you choose to greet the day with a stretching ritual, take time over breakfast for a moment of gratitude, or perform a mindful meditation on your commute, with this book, you'll discover how just a few reverent minutes each morning can imbue you with a sense of peace and purpose to last all day.

Have you enjoyed this book?

If so, why not write a review on your favourite website?

If you're interested in finding out more about our books, find us on Facebook at Summersdale Publishers, on Twitter/X at @Summersdale and on Instagram, TikTok and Bluesky at @summersdalebooks and get in touch. We'd love to hear from you!

Thanks very much for buying this Summersdale book.

www.summersdale.com

## IMAGE CREDITS

p.6 and throughout
© YEVHENIIA BUNHA/Shutterstock.com;
p.11 and throughout © sini4ka/Shutterstock.com